A Creative PATH Through Breast Cancer

My Story in Collage and Poetry

ARELLA TOMLINSON

A Creative Path Through Breast Cancer: My Story in Collage & Poetry

by Arella Tomlinson
www.arellatomlinsonart.com

Published by Resting Space Books
Monrovia, California USA
info@restingspacebooks.com
www.restingspacebooks.com

ISBN: 979-8-218-09159-0 (paperback)
ISBN: 979-8-218-09164-4 (ebook)

Cover and layout by Heather UpChurch, www.artanddesignstudios.net
Editing by Emilie Parker

This book is dedicated to my grandmothers, Betty and Lenora, who were also Breast Cancer Survivors, my artist mother, Emilie Parker, who taught me that making art is for everyone, and my Art Therapy professors at Loyola Marymount University.

Acknowledgments

I am so grateful to my husband Justin Tomlinson, who's daily blood, sweat, and tears supported me through all of this, and to his wonderful parents. To my loving and talented mom Emilie Parker who helped me in writing and editing. Thanks to Heather UpChurch for her beautiful book design. I also appreciate my awesome healthcare team at Kaiser Permanente. To my supportive co-workers there in public health and web publishing, you helped me more than you realize. To my entire Karspeck, Parker, and Tomlinson families who have encouraged and supported me, thank you! And lastly, I'm grateful to God, whose hand catches me, and whose spirit co-creates with me.

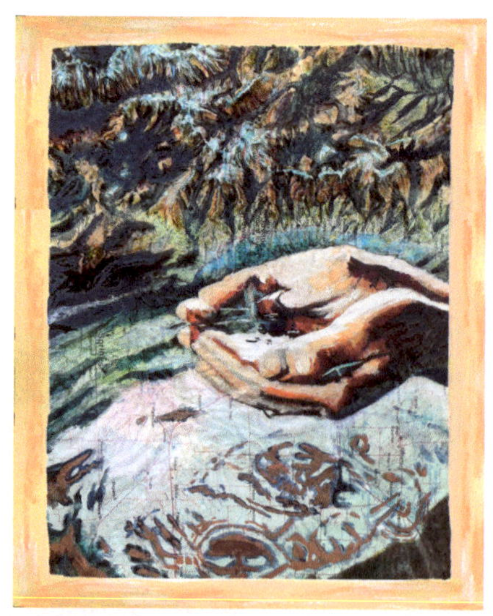

Contents

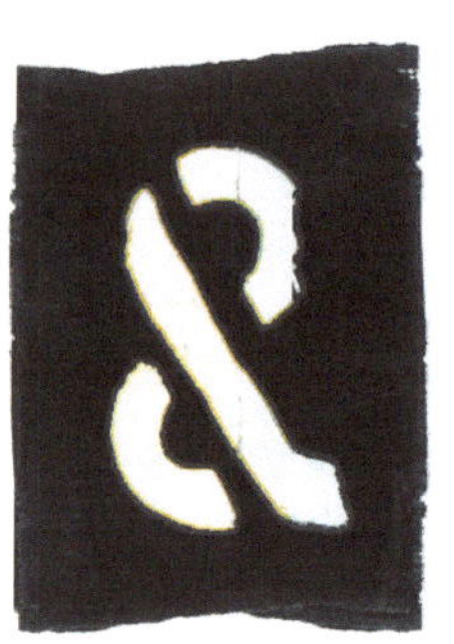

Introduction

This collection, created in 2014 and 2015, is about my experience of finding a breast lump and then undergoing lumpectomy, chemotherapy, and radiation treatments for breast cancer. At the time it all started I was a new mom to my 6-month-old baby boy. Making these collages, and their accompanying poems, served as a personal therapeutic process for me. It was a way to document and sort through the confusion and constant questioning. It was a way to bear the emotional and physical discomforts. It helped me in my search for meaning and provided me a creative path through it all.

When I showed this art in a local gallery, I called the show “Residual Tenderness.” That's what I feel when I review my path through breast cancer. I chose “Residual” because some of the physical and emotional scars from the experience have stayed with me to this day. I chose the word “Tenderness”, because I feel tenderness for those who go through cancer themselves, and for those who go through it with loved ones. My wounds have generated compassion. I feel it for you, my friends, as you are finding your own path through hardships.

I hope you enjoy this collection and find it meaningful to you.

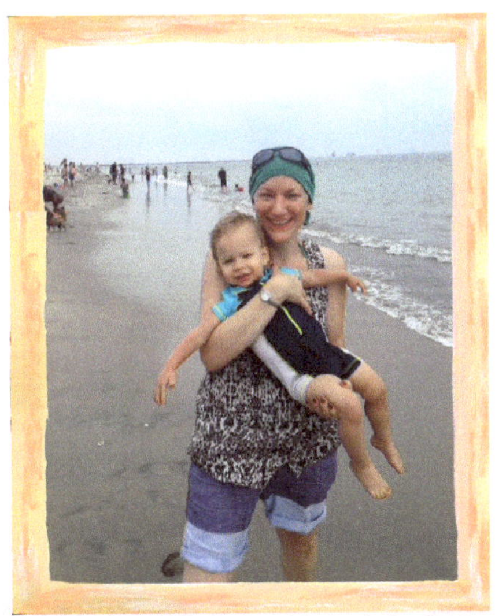

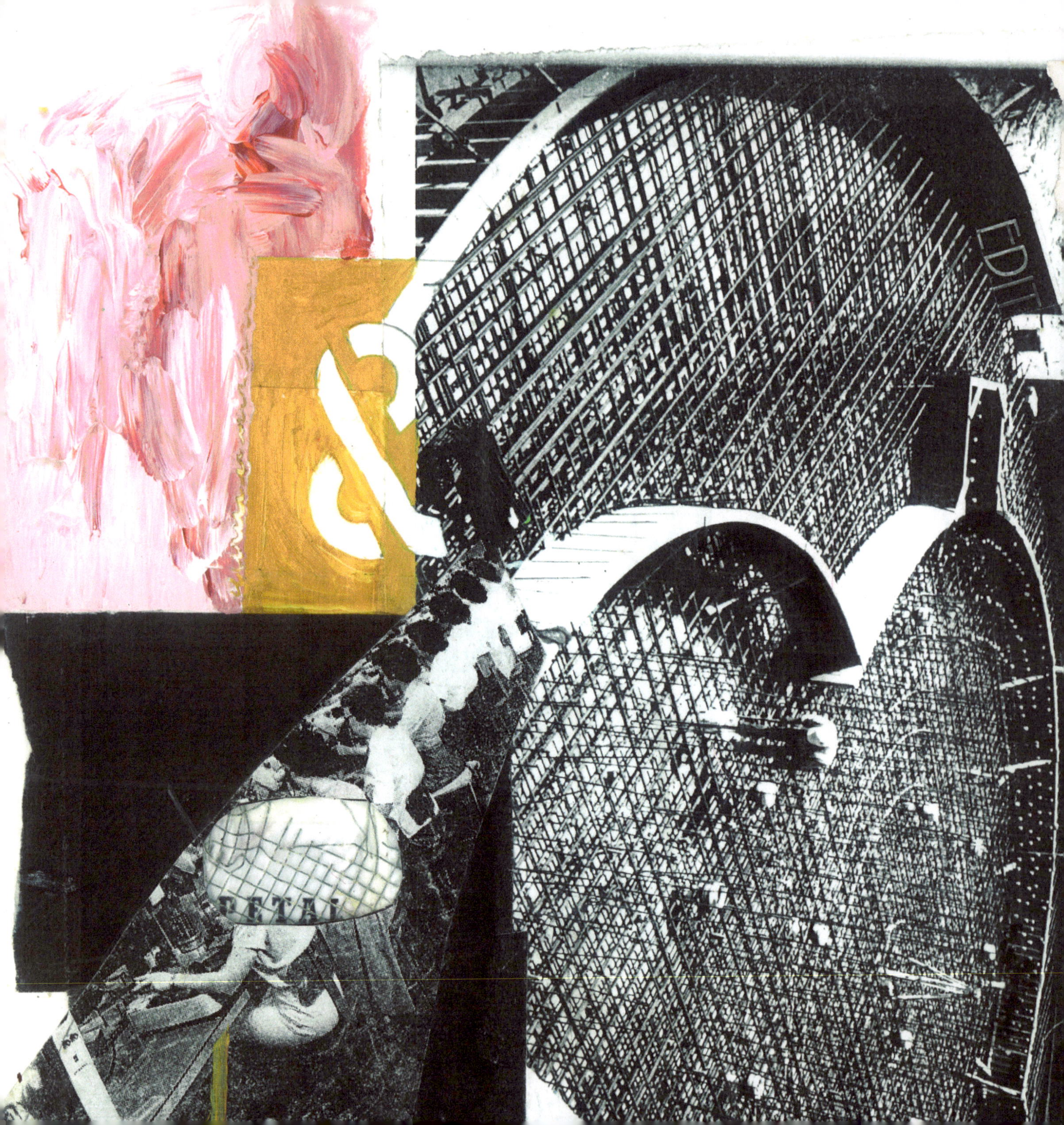
&
EDIT

Petal

A routine self-screening was
slightly askew,
But when I called it in, I wasn't
expecting this.
This.
To be called and told that I have it,
To be called out to join
One in eight American women.
I thought,
Can I step back in line and wake up
And this never will have happened?
And this the same day that my baby
crawled for the first time.

Oh, soft petal...
Its spring
Yet I fear that You, precious new
(& so close to my heart)
Will be plucked away.

I feel picked
To walk the plank
As if scaffolds of cold steel are
rising up around me
Squeezing me onto a grid
Editing Me out
Filtering fleshiness to replace with fear.

It feels like
The Lump
Is in my throat.
If only I could swallow it back down.

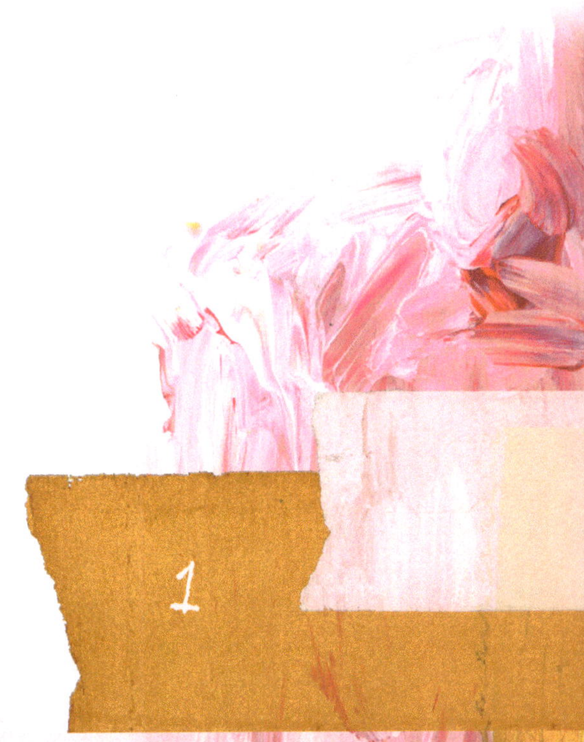

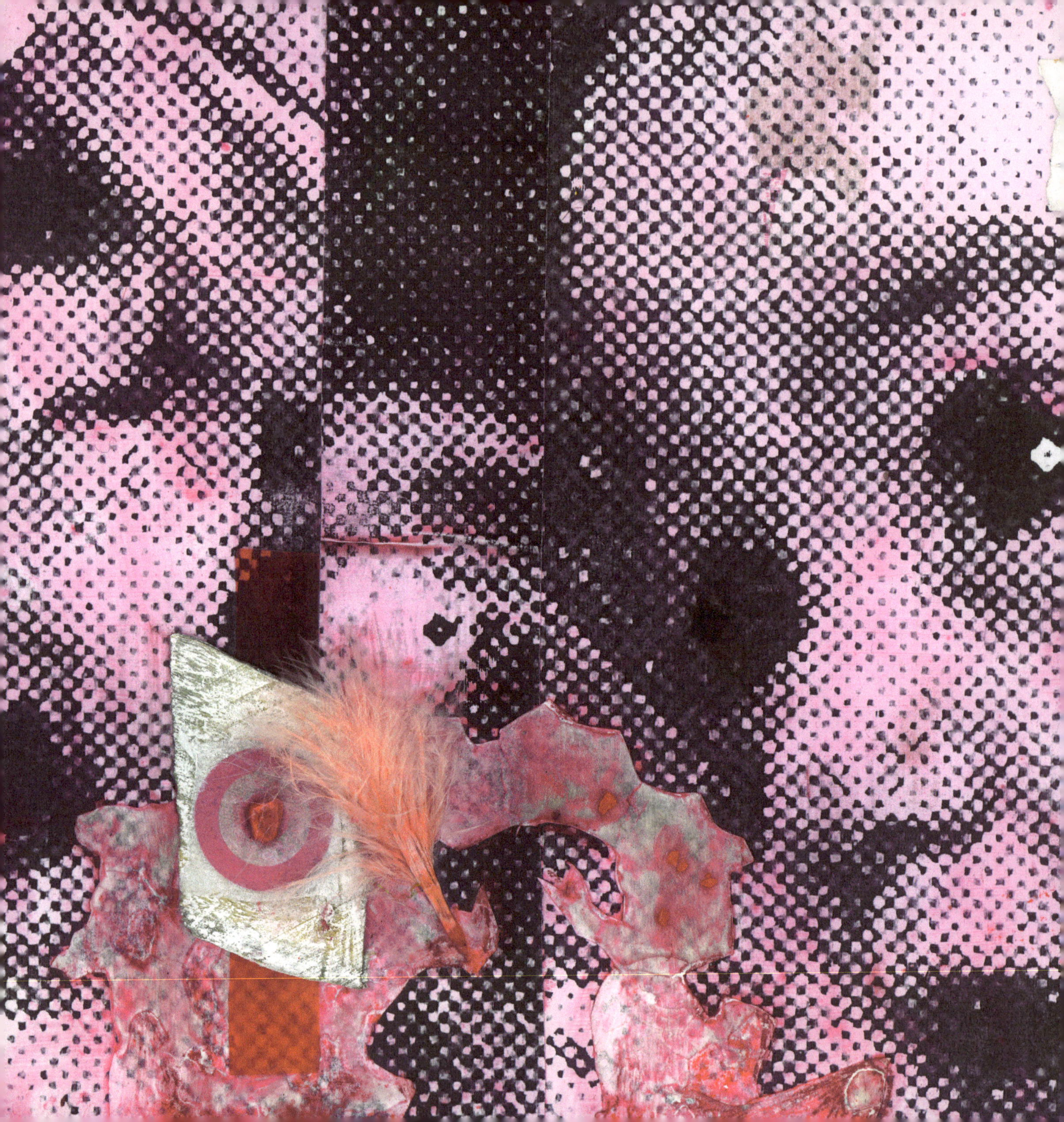

Mammo Mama

¡Ouch!
I feel like the target
Of so much squishing and squeezing,
Ordered and served up
On the cold platter of this
screening machine,
State-of-the-art-my-xxx,
That is checking for more lumps,
Before I go under the knife.

Hold still, says the steely worker
woman,
So I squirm inside, thinking – I hope
you feel sorry for me,
Yes, I am so young
And breastfeeding.

What do they mean I have to
Quit (almost) cold-turkey, for the surgery
And how?
Out come the last few drops of
nourishment
Onto the metal plate.

Bye bye, littleness of my baby.
This new flow of life
Cut off unexpectedly, for both of us.

It was like nesting, nestling,
Like the soft sound of feathers rustling.
And shhhhh, precious one...
His head fit so perfectly in the crook
of my right arm.

Rooting, we rock, but are coming up dry.

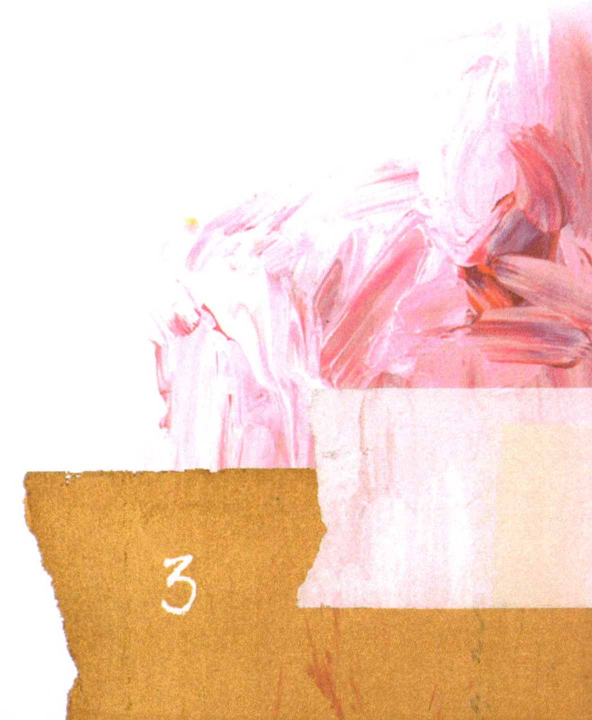

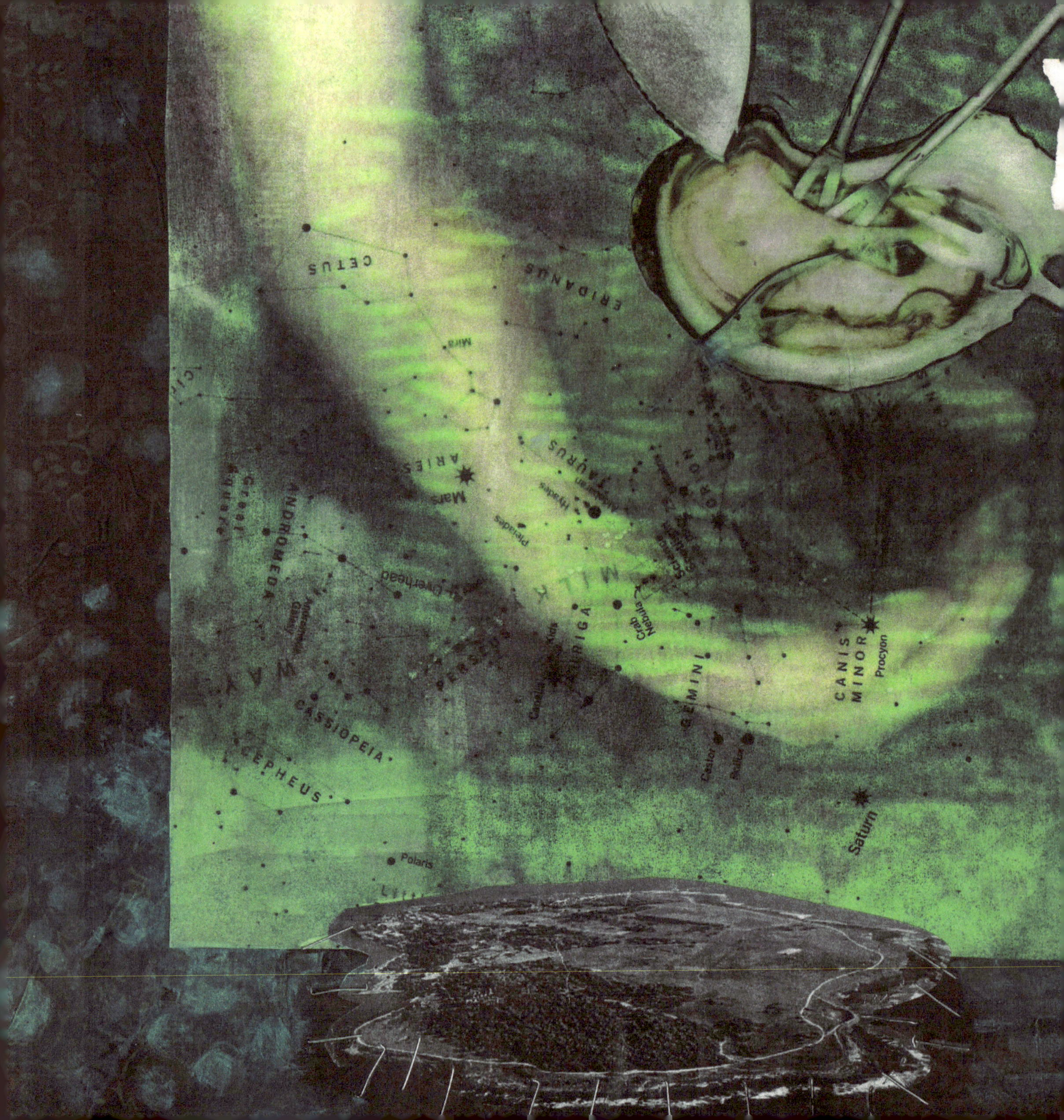

CETUS
ERIDANUS
Mira
TAURUS
ARIES
Mars
Hyades
Pleiades
ANDROMEDA
MILKY WAY
Overhead
ORION
Crab Nebula
AURIGA
PERSEUS
CASSIOPEIA
CEPHEUS
GEMINI
Castor
Pollux
CANIS MINOR
Procyon
Saturn
Polaris

Fear

The surface of my skin appears so still—
No ripples, intact.
So how can it be that it will be
Breached
And (if it could be felt) like
Some Unspeakable Invasion
And a part of me, the lump, removed?
And do I want them wide (or would I
rather keep) all my Margins?

An untenable compromise must
be reached,
Myself agreeing, for the first time,
To be utterly powerless In someone
else's hands
Which may be skilled,
But nevertheless, are holding a knife.

Surrounded by offers of support
And yet I still feel
Like a defenseless creature,
even without bones
On an Island.

My own hand (and maybe the Divine?)
reaches down
Gentle, cupping
To steady this storm
And it works, partially.

But cleaning and rubbing the
preparatory solution on my body,
I still wonder,
Will I see myself on the other side?

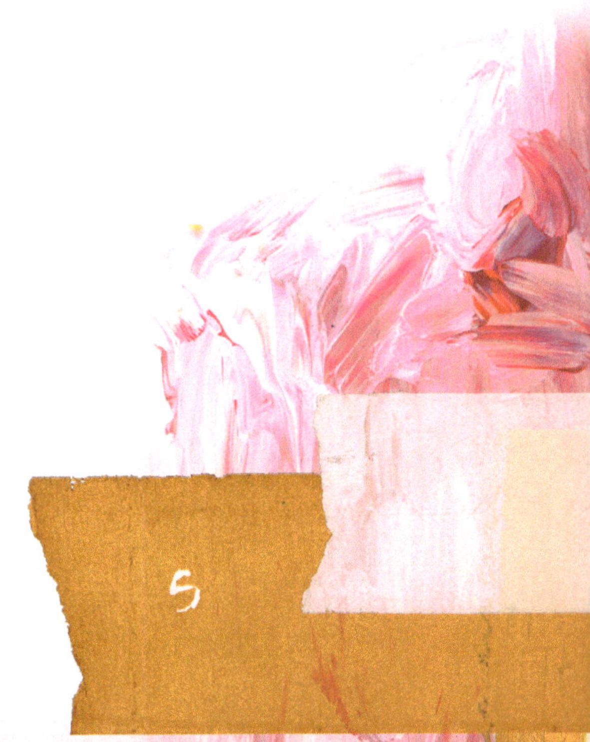

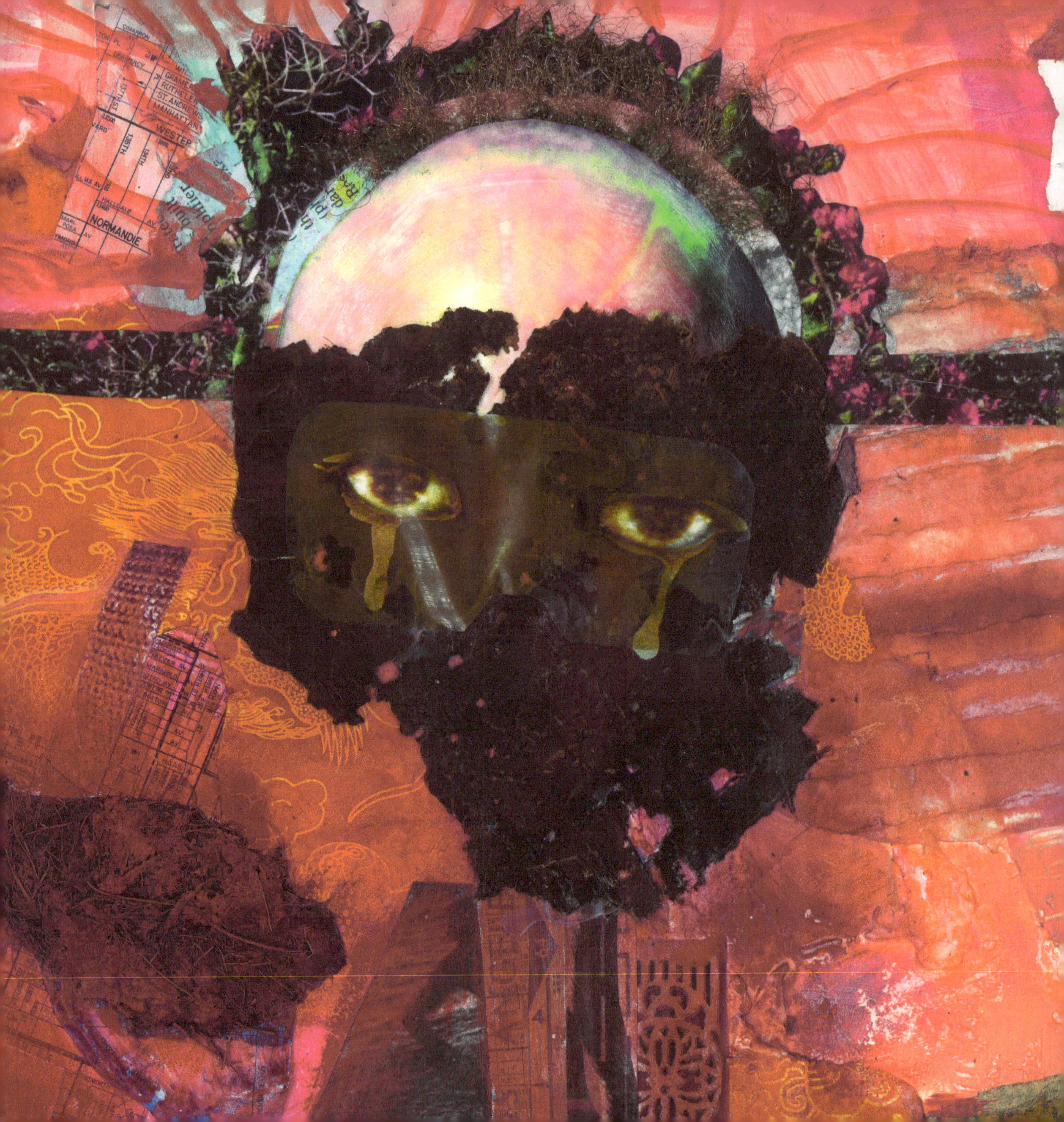
CIMARRON
RUTHELEN
ST. ANDREWS
MANHATTAN
WESTER
137TH ST
135TH
134TH
ALMA AV
HALLDALE
NORMANDIE
MARIPOSA

Dawn of Suffering

Way too slick, it slithers up
Uninvited though reluctantly expected.
I wince.
A toxic flush has given birth... To a new
Me, On a (hot) new morning.
I cannot stop sweating.

Chosen
To stick out like a sore,
To carry this banner of leprosy.
Branded,
having to sport 'The Look',
To radiate exposure to the dreaded 'C',
That we we we would rather not think
of and I I I would rather not be, and
have to cover.
Selected
To reflect the utter lack
Of all softness and fringe,
A beacon for the coming Anti-Comfort.

But since it is here anyway, I'll say...

Good morning, Lion-without-his-mane
Rise, Eel-of-my-nightmares-sans-
eye-brows...

Go ahead and amplify my barrenness
In Sampson's vein,
But at least help me figure out
What color of scarf
Will match today's apology.

Is it vain to complain of
This crown of thorns to
My young, thriving soul?

So much more than an annoyance,
This Easter Morning
Was no holiday
This day is when
It felt real.

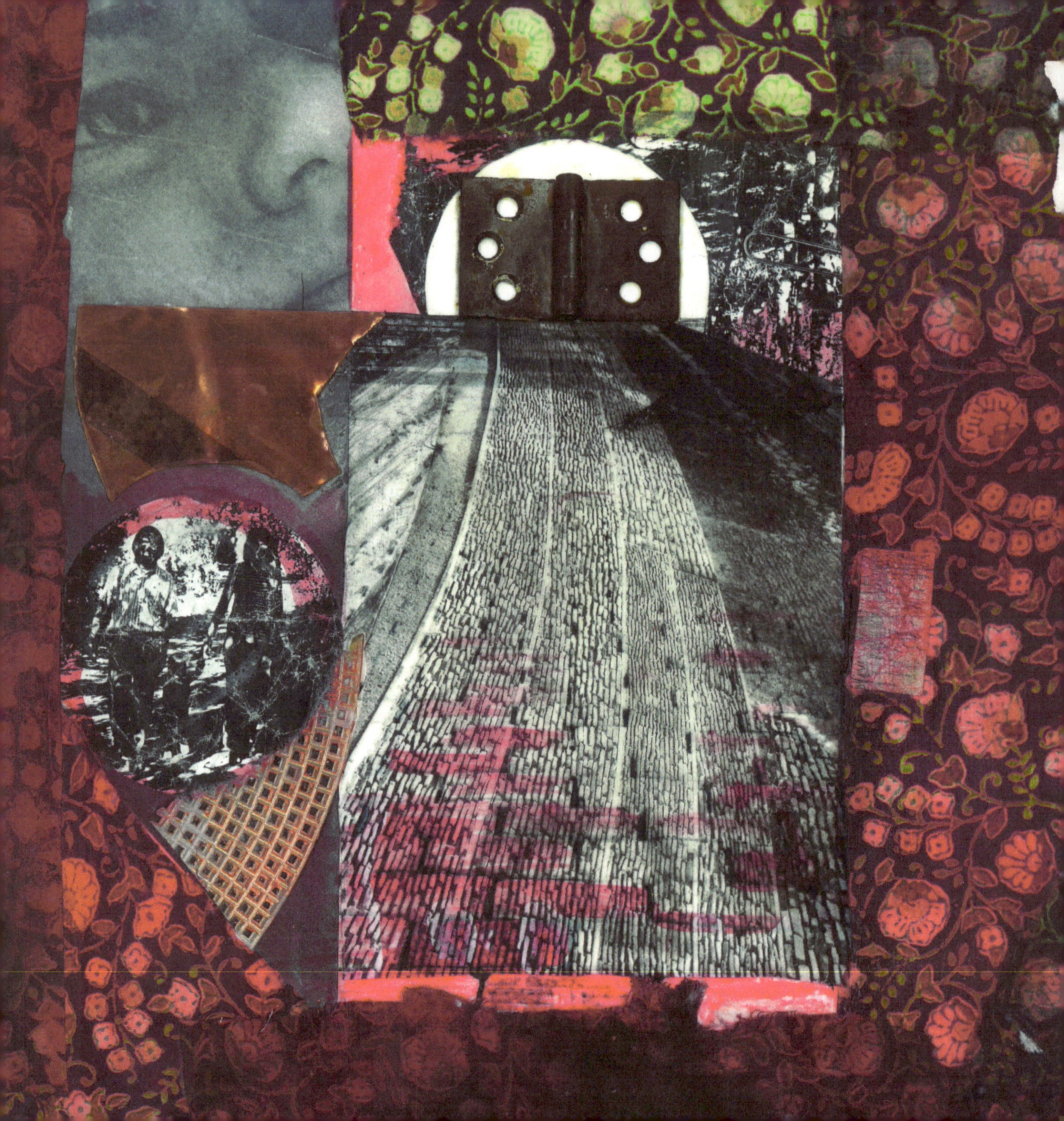

Long Road, Weary Legs, Heavy Door

Like a child, learning to step
I started the journey.

I know it sounds strange
But at first I felt so optimistic and
blessed even proud
To be surviving so well.
I strolled us around my neighborhood
briskly with a
Euphoric (almost manic) smile.

But then came
The monthly yuck,
The scheduled misery, 4 days,
The hot mess,
The anticipation of the next marathon
to hit my legs,
And the pills, appointments, hot
flashes, and hives
And walking on pins and needles... It
all made me feel older.

Where does this long road lead?

And slowly it became
Admittedly, too much,

Meanwhile "doing fine" socially,
because Ego is such a great cope-er,
My legs were alone to wonder... Is it
safe to just BUCKLE?
To come completely UN-HINGED?
And someone(s) would catch me, so
they say??

"Not yet!", the Heavy Door boomed,
Slamming me further shut,
Yet calling me to continue on.

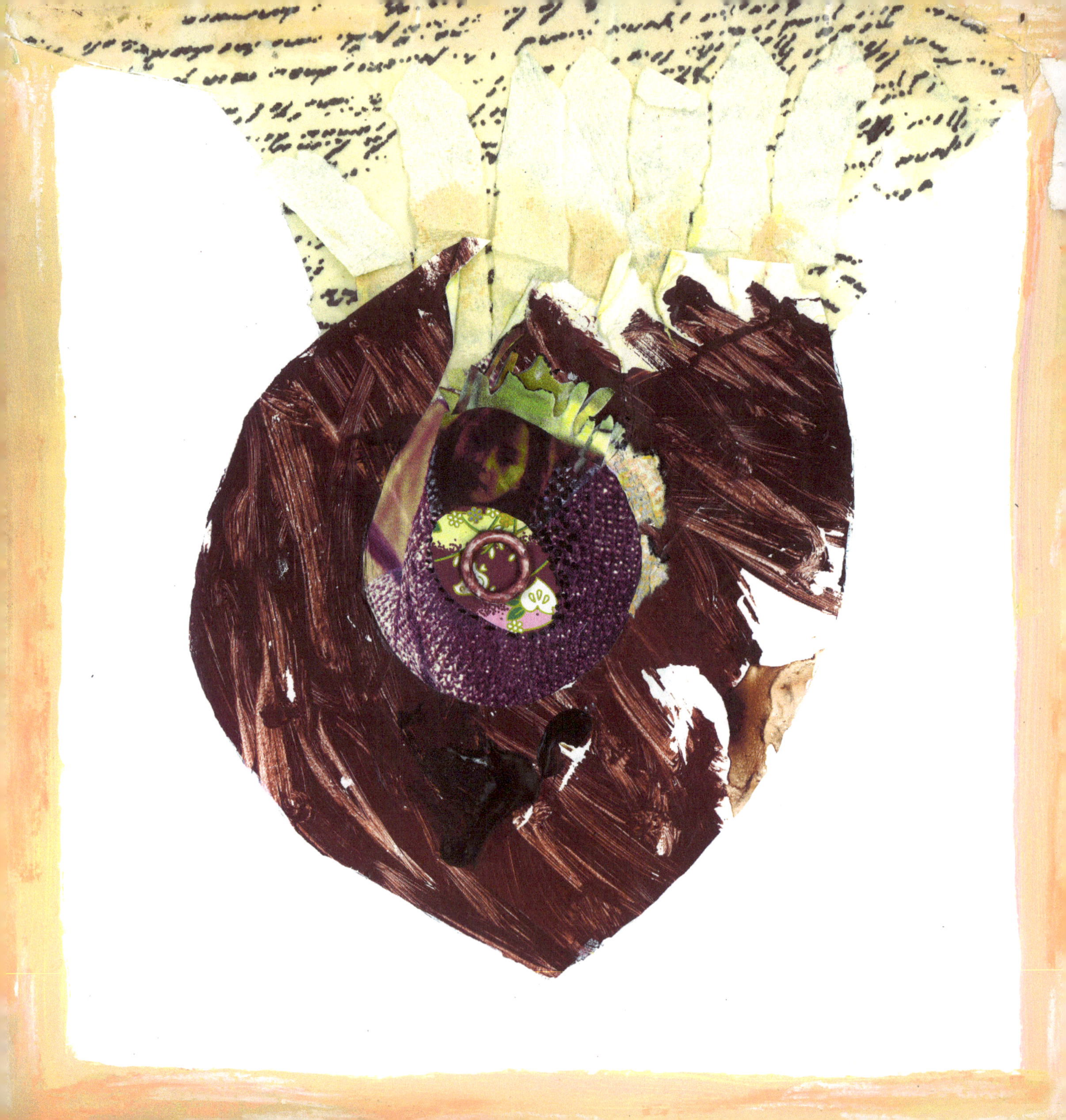

Sacred Heart

With tenderness, she had proclaimed:
It will feel like your skin is still burning
for two weeks after,
after the end. And let us hope the
tingling in your feet will go away.

Now, at this completion of sorts
As my body has quite suddenly been
deemed safe,
I exhale, but not deeply.
I try to steady my eyes, which dart to
the corners
Yet gloss over the shadows
And hesitate to look back.

But, during one of the few still
moments I could allow,
Staring forward, peering into this frame,
I waited for something to appear:
A reason, a summation, maybe a
grand symbol,
Or at least a recipe
For some type of sweet starter,
Some golden nugget
Wrapped in phyllo or rice paper
To ready my stomach for this digestion.
Something to guide me so slowly inside
Something that will help me either to
Ravel up or to unravel
Whichever will lead to rest,
And I have no idea which...
During this confounding puzzle
Of torn pieces, these unsorted bits
of rubble.

Then, a simple image emerged...
The symbol of a flaming heart,
Quietly burning, refining,
Holding treasure:
My persevering pristine Self -
An ember contained yet erupting,
Sparking tongues that speak volumes,
That blot gently at my real wounds,
Refining and providing a
way to begin
This after.

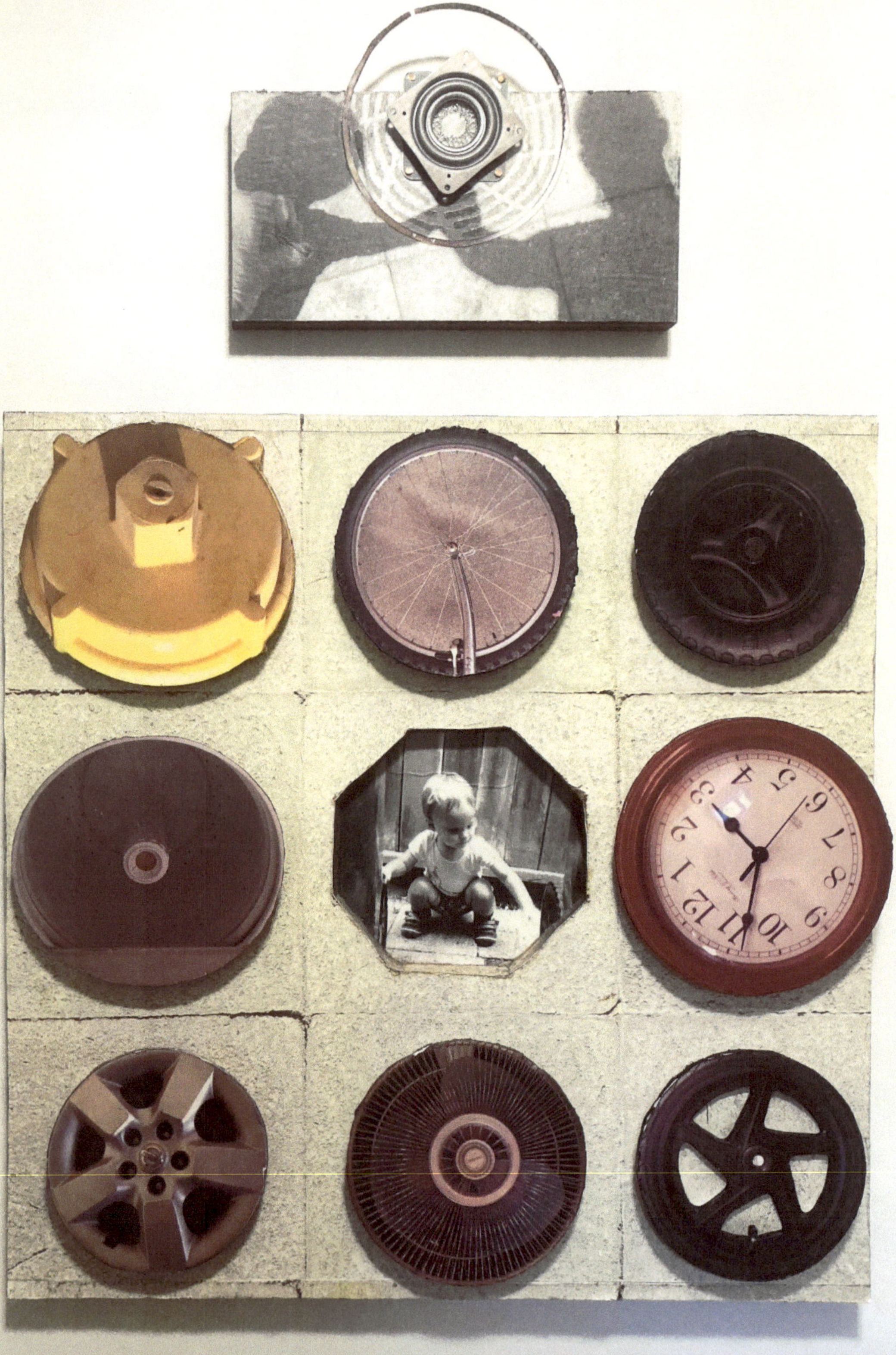

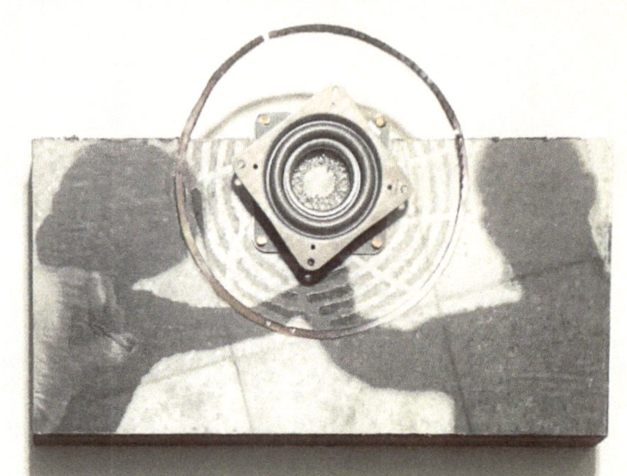

Wheels and We: The Silver Lining

"Please twirl," would say their sign.
"Go ahead. Right now!
We urge you to get down and let us
roll."

These wheels of whimsy
These whirring disks
Are and were, for me,
About the Nows of those 8 months
Of spending time with my baby.

My being sick and off work, afforded
us this time.

The keeping of motion
Which keeps on discovering
The round joy of
Millions of household (and
neighborhood)
Moments together,
Mmmmm...

To overlap all of our circles,
To play and not to part,
To trace the end to its start,
To stroll our loops, listening to birds
and making favorite sounds.
Touching every hedge, turning over
every rock.
To jump and chase shadows,
To spin in the grass, or on the old
concrete patio, if we dare.
To orbit, on cloud 9, during his first steps,
And for me just to know every little
and big interest,
Like this one, the wheels, the circles,
That my emerging energetic toddler
Loves loves loves.

This turn of our events.
It well made up for the trials.

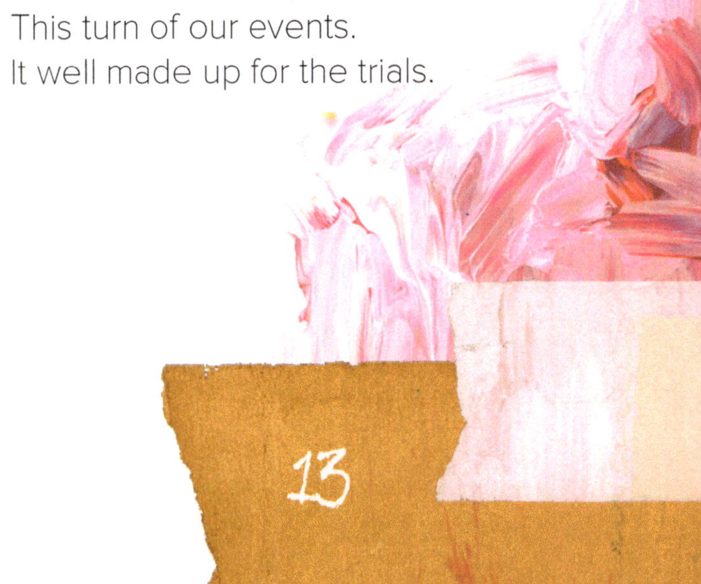

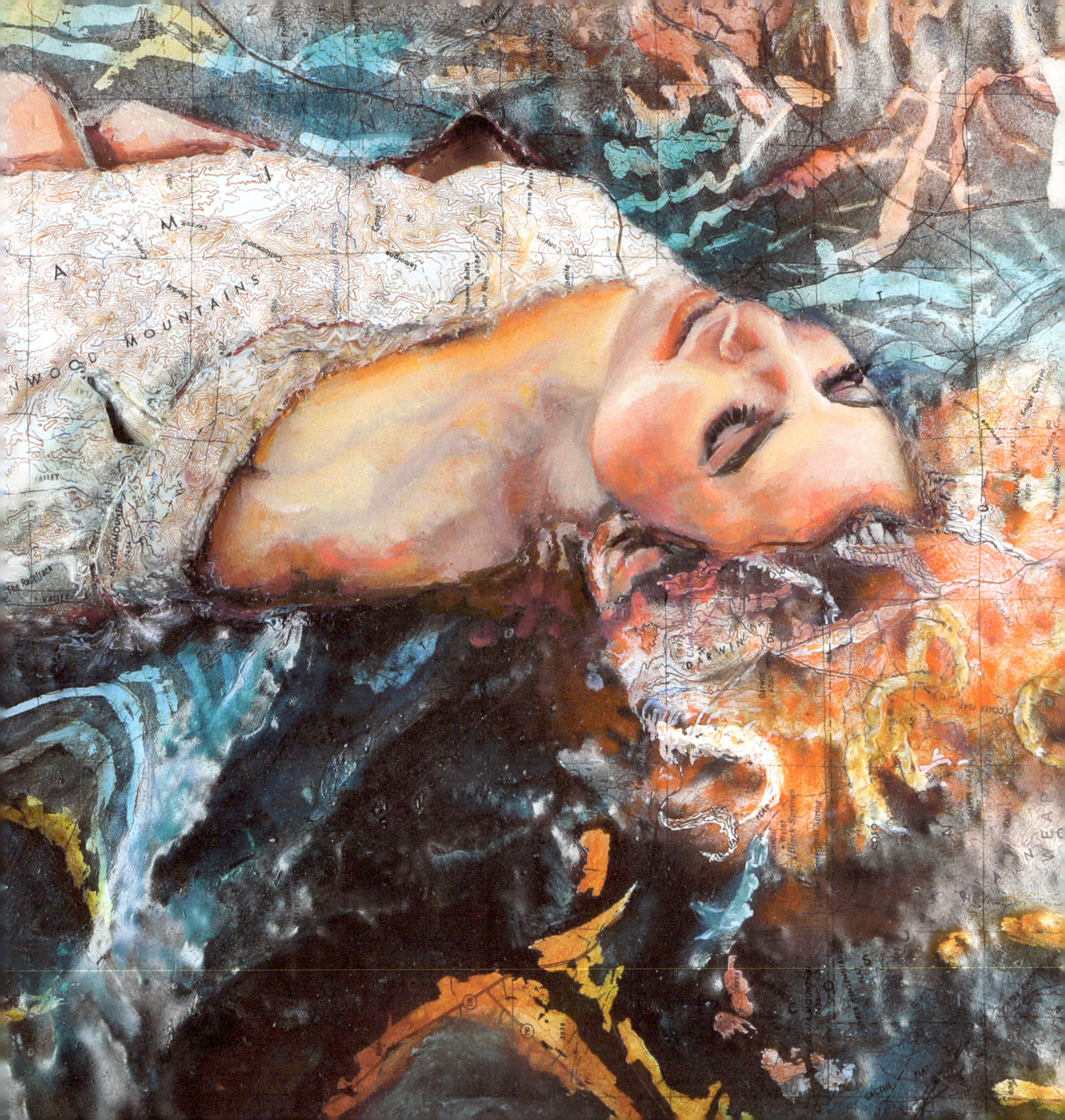
NWOOD MOUNTAINS
DARWIN

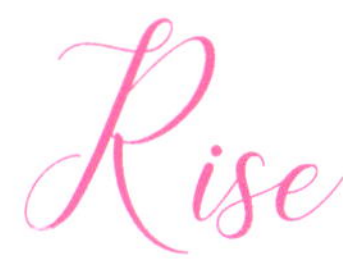

Rise

And the path itself was a treasure
in her pocket.
She had layed down fears,
Dutifully re-assigned to-do's,
To create,
Without self judgement.
And rest came.

The creations came alive, making roads, making rivers around the mountains.
She remembered the love that surrounded her the whole time. She had never been alone.

Wrapped. Floating over the land,
Over the mountains,
Over the waves,
It is her Rebirth.

She is cared for and brought back to a higher place.

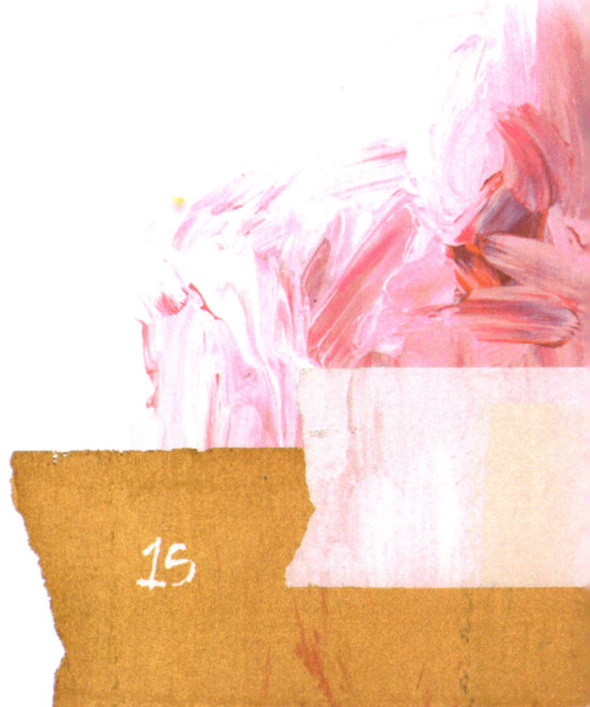

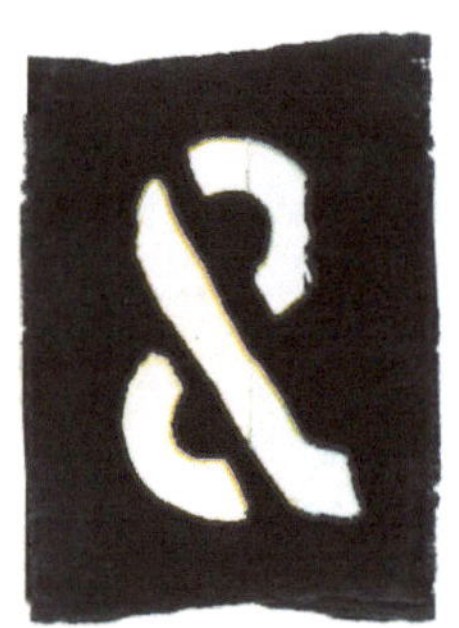

Note from the Author

I would be so thrilled to hear from you! Please feel free to contact me. I'd like to hear anything and everything about you, or how you liked the book!

arella@arellatomlinsonart.com

About the Author

Arella Tomlinson is a mixed-media artist who lives with her husband and 2 children and has her art studio in the Los Angeles area. She is currently working on a series of figurative and abstract paintings on top of collaged topographical maps. As a breast cancer survivor with a bachelors in fine arts and a masters in art therapy, Arella is sharing her creative collage and poetry process with others in hopes that they will be inspired to use their creativity to help themselves cope with life's challenges and to heal from them. Connect with her online at www.arellatomlinsonart.com, Instagram @arella_tomlinson, Facebook @arellat, and TikTok @arella_tomlinson. Art prints are available.

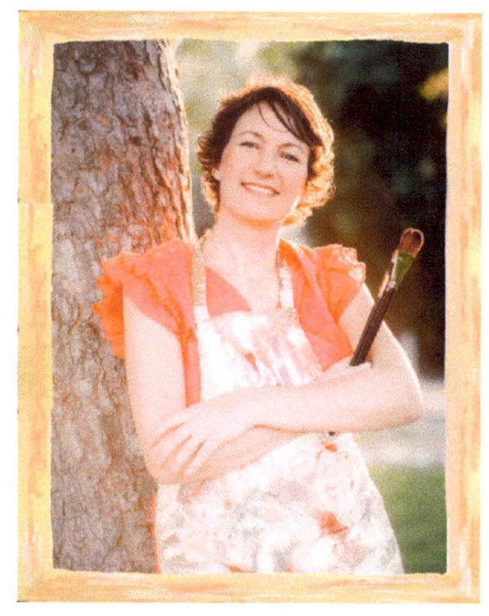

www.ingramcontent.com/pod-product-compliance
Lightning Source LLC
LaVergne TN
LVHW070207110826
845147LV00002B/529

* 9 7 9 8 2 1 8 0 9 1 5 9 0 *